FINDING
YOUR PURPOSE

Becoming all you
were meant to be

YOUTH WITH A MISSION

ZondervanPublishingHouse
Grand Rapids, Michigan

A Division of HarperCollinsPublishers

GET CONNECTED!
Living Encounters Series

Finding Your Purpose
Copyright © 2000 by Youth With A Mission

Requests for information should be addressed to:

📖 ZondervanPublishingHouse
Grand Rapids, Michigan 49530

ISBN 0-310-22702-X

The Living Encounters Bible study series was produced through a dynamic team process of Youth With A Mission staff members, although each guide was created by one primary author. The team consisted of: Betty Barnett, Retha Badenhorst, Maureen Menard, Ruth Perrin, Ed Sherman, Donna Jo Taylor, and Christine Terrasson. The primary author of Finding Your Purpose *was Ed Sherman with Ruth Perrin.*

Interior design by Sherri Hoffman

Printed in the United States of America

02 03 04 05 /❖ EP/ 10 9 8 7 6 5

Contents

foreword
Close Encounters with the Living God

Welcome to the Living Encounters Bible study series! We created this unique study to help sincere seekers find a deeper revelation of God. Our God loves to be pursued. He wants us to know and love him more, and there's no better way to learn of his character and his ways than through his written Word.

The Living Encounters series offers exciting new ways for you to engage Scripture and apply its truth to your life. Through this series, each participant is encouraged into living encounters with God, his Spirit, his Word, his people, and his world.

Some elements of the study are drawn from teaching methods that have been used for decades in our Discipleship Training Schools. As our students encounter God, their perspective on life changes radically. The very truth of the Scripture connects them to the global picture, to God's heart for the peoples of the world. Therefore, the more they come to know God, the more they want to make him known.

The Living Encounters series is a wonderful Bible study tool for people of various levels of spiritual maturity. Its flexible, user-friendly format appeals to people with different learning styles and cultural perspectives. And when coupled with the teaching aids found in the Christian Growth Study Bible (Zondervan), the series is a highly effective way to draw new understanding and guidance from the Scriptures.

May this series bring you a whole new appreciation of our awesome God—and set you on the pathway to many living encounters!

—Loren Cunningham,
Founder of Youth With A Mission

Introducing Living Encounters

Did you ever hear about a person you'd never met—what he said, what he looked like, what he did—and then you met him, and somehow the picture you had formed in your mind didn't fit at all? For better or worse, you were confronted with reality! An "encounter" does not mean a secondhand report about a person or a situation; it means a face-to-face meeting. In an encounter, you meet a person, and your knowledge about him or her combines with and adapts to the living reality.

This is what "Living Encounters" is all about. You have read God's Word, the Bible, but there is a gap between what it says and what you experience. You know God's Spirit is alive and well, but life would be a lot simpler if he sat down beside you and gave you advice. You like people, but sometimes loving them seems impossible. And then there's the whole world out there—so full of need and suffering that you don't know how to even begin to help.

Living Encounters are more than an analysis of Bible passages or a tool for group discussion. They are to help you *meet* and adjust your life to God's Word, God's Spirit, God's people, and God's world. They are designed to challenge you not only to grasp truth but to live it out, to connect it to your personal world and to the larger world around you. As you apply yourself to these studies, you can expect exciting changes both in your thinking and in your lifestyle.

The Living Encounters series is versatile. Each guide is divided into six sessions and can be used within a small-group discussion in a church or on a college campus. However, the series is designed so that it is just as effective for individual study.

The guides are personal. They constantly lead you to ask, "What does this mean to me and how do I apply it in my own life?" Questions reveal needs and desires of the heart and invite you to embrace the promises, assurances, exhortations, and challenges of God's Word. As you respond, the Spirit of God will be responding to you, renewing your mind and transforming you more into the likeness of Jesus Christ—the ultimate goal of all Bible study.

The Features

Each session includes the following basic features.

Opening Vignette

To draw you into the topic at hand, each session opens with a thought-provoking narrative.

Preparing Heart and Mind

These questions open your heart and focus your mind on what God wants to say to you in the passage. If you are using Living Encounters in a group setting, we strongly encourage you to include this section during the first fifteen minutes of your discussion. Please realize, however, that the entire study will probably take about an hour and fifteen minutes. If you don't have that much time, then ask your group members to reflect on these questions before you meet together, and begin your discussion with the section "Engaging the Text."

Setting the Stage

The background information found in this sidebar will help you better understand the context of the study.

Engaging the Text

This important section leads you through a Bible passage using inductive Bible study questions. The inductive method prompts you to observe, interpret, and apply the Bible passage with a variety of question styles:

- **Observation questions** will help you focus on what the Bible says.
- **Interpretation questions** will help you step into the world of the original readers to understand better what the passage meant to them.
- **Application questions** will help you to apply the truth to your heart and present circumstances.

Responding to God

In this section, you will receive suggestions that will help you focus your individual or group prayer time.

Punch Line

This brief sentence or verse will reinforce the theme of the session.

Taking It Further

This section is designed to be completed between studies to reinforce and further apply what you have learned. It offers a variety of suggestions for connecting what you have studied to your everyday life.

- **Connecting to Life:** a variety of activities to stimulate your personal growth and ministry to others.
- **Digging Deeper:** additional Scriptures to give a deeper and broader understanding of what the Bible says about the topic of the study.
- **Meditation:** a time to reflect more deeply on a specific verse or passage.
- **Personal Expression:** creative suggestions to help you process and apply what you've learned in the session.
- **World Focus:** an encouragement to look beyond your personal realm to the needs of our world.

Additional Features

In addition to the above, the guides contain a variety of optional features. All are designed to appeal to different learning styles and gifts and to encourage deeper integration of material into all of life. It is expected that you will choose whatever features you find most useful for each session. These optional features, found in articles throughout the sessions, include:

- **Gray boxed material:** devotional articles relevant to the study.
- **People of Impact:** a snapshot of the life of a person who models the principles studied.
- **People Profile:** a brief description of a people group that needs to be reached with the gospel.
- **Hot Topic:** a discussion starter to use with other group members to stimulate deeper thinking on a difficult subject.

Leader's Notes

Leader's notes for each session are provided at the back of each study guide.

Suggestions for Individual or Group Study

Preparing Heart and Mind

1. Ask the Lord for insight, wisdom, and grace to understand the Bible passage and apply it to your own life.
2. Choose one or more of the preparation questions and take time to think about it.

Engaging the Text

1. Read and reread the assigned Bible passage. You may find it helpful to have several different translations. A good literal translation rather than a paraphrase is recommended, such as the *New International Version*, the *New American Standard Bible*, the *New Revised Standard Version*, and the *New King James Bible*. The questions in each study are based on the *New International Version*. A Bible dictionary can also serve you well for look-

ing up any unfamiliar words, people, places, or theological concepts. Commentaries, while having great value, are not part of this kind of study, which uses the inductive method.

2. The questions are designed to help you make observations, draw conclusions, and apply God's truth to your life. Write your answers in the space provided. Recording your observations and conclusions is an important step in any study process. It encourages you to think through your answers thoroughly, thus furthering the learning process.

3. Note the optional elements offered in the sidebars. These are designed to encourage greater understanding of the passage being studied.

4. Be aware of the continuous presence of the Lord throughout the process. You may want to stop and pray in the midst of your study. Be sure to end your study with a time of waiting, listening, and responding to the Lord in prayer.

5. Be willing to participate in the discussion. The leader of the group will not be lecturing; rather, he or she will be encouraging the members of the group to discuss what they have learned from the passage. The leader will be asking the questions that are found in this guide. Plan to share what God has taught you in your individual study time.

6. Stick to the passage being studied. Your answers should be based on the verses which are the focus of the discussion and not on outside authorities such as commentators or speakers (or the commentary notes in your study Bible!).

7. Be sensitive to other members of the group. Listen attentively when they share. You can learn a lot from their insights! Stick with the topic — when you have insights on a different subject, keep it for another time so the group is not distracted from the focus of the study.

8. Be careful not to dominate the discussion. We are sometimes so eager to share that we leave too little opportunity for others to contribute. By all means participate, but allow others to do so as well.

9. Expect the Holy Spirit to teach you both through the passage and through other members of the group. Everyone has a unique perspective that can broaden your own understanding. Pray that you will have an enjoyable and profitable time together.

10. The "Responding to God" section is the place where you pray about the topics you have studied. At this time you will invite the Holy Spirit to work these truths further into each of your lives. Be careful not to overlook this essential aspect of your time together.

Taking It Further

1. Identify other questions that arise through the study so that you can pursue them later.

2. Choose one or more of the activities to help you apply the principles in your life. These are optional activities to be done on your own after the Bible study session.

Leader's Notes

If you are the discussion leader or simply want further information, you will find additional suggestions and ideas for each session in the Leader's Notes in the back of this guide.

Finding Your Purpose: Becoming all You Were Meant to Be

The different pieces of Joy's life didn't seem to be fitting together very well. She liked her job as a social worker. At church she taught in the adult Sunday school class. She was part of a local basketball team and enjoyed a busy social life. But what bothered Joy was that the "religious" parts of her life seemed to have little to do with the other parts. What relevance did church or God have to the rest of her world?

As she studied characters in the Bible, this did not seem to be the way things were designed to be. Joy kept noticing that there was a wholeness, a "connectedness," in the lives of the people she read about in the Scriptures. God was involved in every facet of their lives, and they seemed to expect it! They talked to him about all manner of things. He guided their decisions, he changed their hearts, he was with them in their sufferings, and—what struck Joy more than anything else—it seemed that each person had a purpose, a destiny, for which God had specifically made him or her. Yes, that's what she wanted! As she caught that vision of what life could be like, she turned to God in prayer. "Please," she asked God, "lead me into the wholeness of life I see in the Scriptures. Please show me the destiny that you have planned for me." Joy's life was never the same again.

Many of us experience life as Joy did. God has his place. We worship regularly and give faithfully to our church and missions. But we don't see much relevance between church or God and the rest of our lives. We choose our professions, arrange our schedules, enjoy our friendships. But all too often we fail to realize that God *really* cares about the things that matter to us, he wants to be involved in all of our decisions, and he has a destiny for us.

The truth is, every part of your life belongs to him, and he longs for you to become all you were meant to be by fulfilling the purposes he created you for. In this series of studies we will look at some of the character qualities God expects in those who follow him; ways in which God speaks to his people; and his purposes in our lives. If your desire is to become more like Jesus, to grow more confident in God's guidance, more sure of his presence in life's difficulties, and more certain of the destiny he has created you for . . .

. . . then this study is for you!

Holiness —— Being Like Him
Ephesians 4:17–5:20

John had always been known among his friends for his filthy language. Every sentence that came out of his mouth was sure to be spattered with curses or swear words. But when he became a Christian, John soon found that there was a change going on inside him. Each time he was about to pepper his conversation with one of his favorite curses, he would suddenly feel uncomfortable, even embarrassed. To his own amazement, he sensed that somehow it was wrong, even though at first he couldn't explain why. Within a very short time his filthy language was a thing of the past. There were other things in his life that God still needed to deal with, but the cursing was gone, and John realized that it was no longer something he wanted to be known for. In fact, what he really wanted was for people to see something of Jesus reflected in his life.

"Be holy, because I am holy."

—— Leviticus 11:44

And that is what God wants! He longs for our lives to show the world what he is like. When people look at us they should see something of the character of the marvelous God we serve. One of his most important qualities is holiness. In order for us to reflect his holiness and enter the destiny God has for us, there are patterns of behavior, learned in the world, that need to be changed. But godly character is not a transformation we can bring about ourselves. Paul's letter to the Ephesians makes it clear that we are "in Christ." This is what makes true change possible, from the inside out. We must depend upon the Holy Spirit to both show us what needs to be changed and to show us how. Sometimes the transformation will come easily and naturally, as it did with John's language. Other things may take longer and involve a struggle, even requiring help from others. But God will enable us to change, to walk in freedom, to show what he is like to the world.

Are there areas of your life in which you still struggle to be more like him? Ask the Holy Spirit to help you change and to give you practical steps you can take to see that happen.

PREPARING HEART AND MIND

- What does the word *holy* bring to your mind?

- Who would you consider to be "holy" people? Why?

engaging the text

setting the stage

- Ephesus is famous in the ancient world for its temple of Diana, where sex with temple prostitutes is part of its worship. Immorality is normal and everywhere.

- Paul started the church in Ephesus on his second missionary journey and has spent three years there to see that it is well established.

Read Ephesians 4:17–32

1. How does the society described by Paul in verses 17–19 compare with the society you see around you today?

2. Paul uses phrases such as "put on" and "put off" (vv. 24–25) to describe how Christians are to live. What does this suggest to you about our part in the process of change?

3. According to verses 25–32, what does Paul say that we must not do, that we must do, and why?

Must Not Do	Must Do	Reasons

4. In which of these areas do you find change difficult? Why?

5. The reasons that Paul gives for these changes are reasons that affect our relationships. In what ways do they do this?

6. What consequences have you seen in your own life and in the world around you of people disobeying Paul's instruction to "not let the sun go down while you are still angry" (v. 26)?

Transforming the Heart

"'For I will take you out of the nations; I will gather you from all the countries and bring you back into your own land. I will sprinkle clean water on you, and you will be clean; I will cleanse you from all your impurities and from all your idols. I will give you a new heart and put a new spirit in you; I will remove from you your heart of stone and give you a heart of flesh. And I will put my Spirit in you and move you to follow my decrees and be careful to keep my laws'" (Ezekiel 36:24–27).

These people seemed hopeless! Despite God's continual goodness and mercy to them, they consistently sought the favor of idols and lived wretchedly sinful lives. God had called Israel to be a reflection of his character to the nations. He wanted all to come to know him. Thankfully, God did not give up. Here he speaks out his plan to create a new humanity, one which could and would reflect him.

Through Jesus, we are recipients of this great promise. In Jesus, God has given us the ability to walk in friendship with him and live according to his standards. Through the cross, our sins can be cleansed and our idols destroyed. He has put within us a new, responsive heart and enabled us to recognize and obey his voice.

We can enter this new life by first seeking to understand who God is and what he has done for us in Jesus Christ. Next, we have to choose to believe this truth and act on it. By obeying God in every circumstance, we can consistently enjoy his indwelling presence and protection.

Write in your own words what God has provided for you to live a holy life.

Read Ephesians 5:1–20

7. The first two verses of chapter 5 summarize what Paul has been saying so far. (Note the "therefore.") What do you think it means to imitate God? How is this possible for us? (See "Transforming the Heart" on page 17.)

8. The world around us affects us, for both good and bad. Paul describes a number of things that should not be found among God's people. Consider your everyday life at home, school, work, and even at church. Where do you come across similar behavior and how does it affect you?

9. What does it mean to be "partners" (v. 7) with those who are doing these things?

Called to Be Accountable

"When he is made aware of the sin he committed, he must bring as his offering a male goat without defect" (Leviticus 4:23).

Al didn't really think of it as accountability when Mark invited him to begin meeting together each week. To him it was simply a time to read the Bible together and talk. Mark began telling his young friend about his personal and spiritual struggles, and soon Al was sharing his own. They talked about relationship problems, spiritual questions, their thought life, and how they were using their time. The result of this "accountability" was strong spiritual growth in both.

It is common to think of accountability as something formal and public, a little like it was experienced in Israel's early history. At that time there was no hope of going unnoticed if you were in trouble. Every time you sinned, you had to take an animal up to the temple as an offering to be sacrificed to the Lord. It was a very visible way of being accountable.

Today relationships of accountability more closely resemble what Al and Mark experienced. Mark created the atmosphere of accountability by sharing freely. Because Al could be open about his struggles, it helped both of them keep moving forward spiritually. Every believer can benefit from this kind of relationship of trust. Friends who regularly share their hearts with one another and pray together will find increasing victory in the Lord.

Have you been accountable to anyone for the growth of your spiritual life? If you'd like such a relationship, ask God to lead you to the right person.

10. Paul encourages the Ephesians to be imitators of God (v. 1). How might *you* imitate God in the situations you are facing, instead of imitating those around you? Try to be specific.

11. Paul describes a strong contrast between what the Ephesians' lives were like before and after coming to know Christ. Your life may be like this, or you may have grown up knowing Christ from childhood, and God has constantly been at work in you. What are the most significant changes he has made in your life?

12. What areas would you still like to grow in?

RESPONDING to GOD

Think of the areas of your life in which you struggle to be holy and bring them before God. Ask him to show you how to become more like him, that is, holy. Ask for practical steps that you can take to work with the Holy Spirit in bringing these areas into line with God's values.

BE IMITATORS
OF GOD, THEREFORE,
AS DEARLY LOVED
CHILDREN.

Ephesians 5:1

taking it further

Suggestions for application

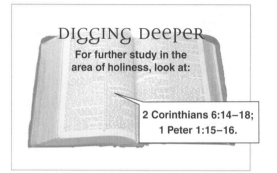

DIGGING DEEPER

For further study in the area of holiness, look at:

2 Corinthians 6:14–18; 1 Peter 1:15–16.

Personal Expression

Be an encouragement! Create a card or write a poem to tell one or two friends of the godly changes that you have seen in their lives.

Meditation

Read 1 Corinthians 6:9–11. Note that Paul is not condemning the Corinthians but reminding them of the amazing truth that they have been cleansed of their past. Take some time to ask God to show you how he sees you and how he sees your areas of weakness and struggles (they will not be the same!). Record them and look back at them from time to time to see how he is working in you.

Connecting to Life

What do you put into your mind? Make a list of all the films, books, music, magazines, and so forth that you have looked at, read, or listened to in the last three months. Divide them into two categories:

1. Those that are uplifting and holy—that put good things into your mind.

2. Those that are unrighteous/unholy—those things that fed junk or sin into your mind.

Consider your list and take some active steps where necessary to improve what you feed your mind.

Contentment and Gratitude——Keys to Peace of Mind
Philippians 3–4

Fleas! They were swarming everywhere. After all the shock and heartache of the last few days, this was the last straw. Back in their family home in Holland, Corrie and Betsy ten Boom had been caught hiding Jews from the Nazis and sent off to the German concentration camp of Ravensbruck. Now they were being pushed through the door of the worst barracks in this infamous camp, filthy, overcrowded, and crawling with fleas. For a moment it seemed too much to bear. Then suddenly to Betsy's mind came the verse in Ephesians, encouraging us always to give thanks to God for everything (Ephesians 5:20). But *this*? In spite of what their minds screamed, the two sisters bowed their heads and thanked God for the fleas.

> **Always giving thanks to God the Father for everything.**
>
> ——ephesians 5:20

Later they discovered an interesting fact: because their barracks was renowned for its plague of fleas, it was the only one the German guards never entered. Betsy and Corrie began to hold Bible studies with their fellow prisoners with no fear of being discovered! Through those times together around God's Word, many of the women came to Christ in what was otherwise a hopeless situation. As they discovered God's purposes, the women found an inner contentment even when surrounded by such terrible circumstances. God was with them!

Giving thanks to God for a situation helps us to recognize that he is involved in it somehow, though we may not understand how. We then begin to see it from God's perspective. He is not responsible for the evil that befalls us, but he has purposes in it which are greater than any disaster. When we realize this, we can cease to rely on our circumstances, or even our own gifts and resources, as the basis for our peace and contentment. All these can change, but God never changes. We find lasting peace and contentment as we learn to look to him.

What difficult situation are you facing? Begin now to give God thanks in the midst of it, trusting that he will use it for good in your life.

PREPARING HEART AND MIND

- Use the following chart to rank your usual first response to a difficult situation. Do you:

	Often	Sometimes	Never
complain?			
quietly endure?			
give thanks to God?			
other? (Specify)			

- Identify a time in your life that you found particularly difficult. Can you see good that came out of it?

engaging the text

setting the stage

- Paul is writing this letter to the Philippians from a prison in Rome.

- Philippi is the site of the first church in Europe, planted by Paul on his second missionary journey (see Acts 16:11–15; 40).

- Paul and Silas were imprisoned and beaten by the city authorities on that first visit (Acts 16:22–23).

- At least one member of the church (the jailer) has heard Paul praise God when in prison after his beating (Acts 16:23–36). The jailer knows the reality that lies behind Paul's words.

Read Philippians 3:1–4:9

1. What do you think Paul means by "confidence in the flesh" (3:3–4)?

2. Identify the things which gave Paul confidence in the flesh before he came to Christ, and the things which might give people confidence in the flesh today, whether they be non-Christian or Christian.

   - Paul:

   - People today:

3. What does Paul now think of these things? Contrast this with what he now gets his confidence from (3:7–14).

4. Even in prison Paul is concerned for others (see 3:18). In difficult circumstances what do you tend to focus on? Be as specific as you can, thinking of concrete examples from your experience.

5. What do you think Paul is referring to when he describes the people in verse 19 of chapter 3?

6. For most of us, there are times when it is easier to look for contentment in earthly things rather than in God. What things do you find are a temptation when looking for contentment?

Embracing the Pain

"Why are you downcast, O my soul? Why so disturbed within me? Put your hope in God, for I will yet praise him, my Savior and my God" (Psalm 42:5–6).

Pain comes as part of the package of life. We can hide it or ignore it. We can wallow in it. Or we can embrace it. Acknowledging and embracing it are the skills of a spiritually healthy person.

In Psalm 42, David comes to grips with his deep pain and discouragement. He remembers better days and exhorts himself to hang on for the good times to come. On several occasions, Jesus also acknowledged and expressed painful emotions. His cry of loneliness from the cross (Matthew 27:46) was the ultimate expression of his personal suffering over our sin.

God wants to touch our spirit in the midst of our deepest pain and loneliness to bring true comfort and hope. He is a loving Father who grieves with us. As we reach out for him, he eagerly responds to us. Countless believers, while suffering deeply, have been sustained by his presence.

Pain can be traumatic—but do not be afraid. God is with you!

Are you able to be real about your pain and simultaneously receive God's comfort? Talk to a close friend about it.

7. What instruction and encouragement for facing difficult times does Paul give his readers in Philippians 4:4–7?

8. Think of a time when you experienced a peace that didn't make sense, when logically you shouldn't have felt peace. What made peace possible?

9. Paul instructs the Philippians concerning the kinds of things they should be thinking about (4:8–9). In what ways do the things you constantly think about help or hinder you when you face difficult circumstances?

Read Philippians 4:10–20

10. Many people experience difficulty in finding contentment where money is concerned. Several elements characterize the attitude of Paul and the Philippians toward finances. What are these elements?

In Love with God, or Money?

"No servant can serve two masters. Either he will hate the one and love the other, or he will be devoted to the one and despise the other. You cannot serve both God and Money" (Luke 16:13).

Money is a useful tool for many good purposes. But Jesus knew that if we began to *love* money, we would soon turn our backs on God. He wants no rivals. We are to love *him* with all our heart, mind, soul, and strength (Mark 12:30).

In 1 Timothy 6:10, the love of money is described as "a root of all kinds of evil." The evidence is all around us: Couples divorce or file bankruptcy because of unwise spending and excessive debt; businesspeople lose hard-earned assets on risky investment schemes; respected citizens are caught cheating on their taxes or stealing from their employers. Love of money drives us to want more than we need and to be filled with fear for the future.

By contrast, God wants us to trust him for our needs and to use whatever wealth he gives us for his purposes. Money in the hands of a Christian can be a powerful weapon for advancing the kingdom of God. Every time we respond in total trust and cheerful generosity, we disarm the spirit of selfishness and greed.

Do you desire to be rich? For what purpose?

11. Describe what might change in your life if you followed their example more closely.

Read Philippians 4:21–23

12. The Philippian jailer came to Christ as a result of Paul's imprisonment in his jail (see Setting the Stage). What do you see in this passage that suggests that Paul's life continued to have an impact in the midst of ongoing difficult circumstances?

Consider a difficult situation which you are facing and in which God may want to use you. Begin by giving God thanks in the midst of it, recognizing that he is with you and expressing faith that he has a purpose for you in it.

give thanks in all circumstances.

1 Thessalonians 5:18

taking it further

Suggestions for application

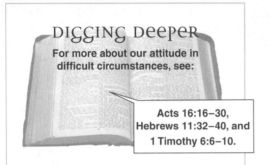

DIGGING DEEPER

For more about our attitude in difficult circumstances, see:

Acts 16:16–30, Hebrews 11:32–40, and 1 Timothy 6:6–10.

Connecting to Life

Make a list of the things which you continually or repeatedly worry about. Keep the list handy and take time every day to pray through it, giving each item to God.

WORLD FOCUS

Pray for a troubling situation (an earthquake, a war, a political scandal) that is currently in the news. Ask God to lead you as you intercede ("Principles for Effective Intercession" on page 96 can help you). Pray particularly that God will bring good out of the situation.

Meditation

Read through Psalm 23. What does it say the Lord will do for us? Why is the psalmist able to be at peace even in the most difficult situations? In what specific ways can you take comfort in the message of this psalm for your own life?

тнат You May Be fruitful
John 15:1–17

Todd couldn't understand what was happening. He had a super girlfriend and had been hoping to marry her; then she broke off the relationship. He was a gifted teacher, but he could find no openings for a permanent position. For months he struggled with one part-time teaching job after another. Friends even suggested that he move to another city to look for work, but he felt sure that the Lord had called him to be where he was. Why then was his life so constricted? Why, if he was doing God's will, were things so painful and frustrating? Where was that "abundant life" Jesus talked about, and where was a fruitful ministry?

Then one day the Lord spoke to him. "You told me you wanted to go deeper with me, Todd," he sensed God saying. "If what you really want is a permanent job, then I'll give it to you. But if your desire truly is to go deeper with me, this is my way to do it." Todd still didn't understand what was happening, but that day he chose to submit to what God was doing and do it his way.

God's will is for us to be fruitful. Our lives are to be a blessing for him, for us, and for others. But some-

> **"I ... appointed you to go and bear fruit—fruit that will last."**
>
> **——JOHN 15:16**

times, in order for us to bear more fruit, we need to go through seasons of pruning. Ministry is reduced. Relationships change. It might feel as if we're being set on the shelf, discarded, overlooked. Yet God's purpose in it all is that we eventually bear more fruit—the result of the work he has done in us through those difficult times. Things happen in our lives that could never have happened without the pruning. God works character and endurance into us, enabling us to receive the blessings he plans to give us.

After several months of part-time jobs, Todd was offered a job in a brand-new school, in much better circumstances than any he could have imagined. In time he met and married a wonderful woman. His life blossomed. Yet he realized that something even more significant had happened: he had come to a new level of perseverance in the face of difficulties and a far deeper trust in God.

PREPARING HEART AND MIND

- "When the Father removes good things from your life, it is punishment for sin." Do you agree with this statement? Why or why not?

- What does it mean to be a friend?

enGaGinG the text

Read John 15:1–17

1. Jesus uses some specific figures of speech, or picture language, concerning himself, the Father, and the disciples. What do these pictures suggest to you about our relationship with the Father?

2. Considering what Jesus says about what happens to the branches that do not bear fruit, how optional do you believe bearing fruit is?

3. Identify a time when the Father was "pruning" your life. Describe the whole process, including your feelings as it was happening. What was the increased fruit he brought about by the pruning?

4. What season do you think you are now in: pruning? bearing fruit?

The Test of the Desert

Beryl couldn't understand why she was suddenly "on the sidelines." A seasoned leader, she loved the action of intense ministry situations. When she sought an answer, the Lord lovingly impressed on her heart: "My strong and capable daughter, I have longed for your fellowship and intimacy, but you are too busy. I have brought you to this place so you might grow in your intimacy with me." Strong in leadership abilities, Beryl needed to be pulled out of her leadership roles for a season in order to allow God to deal with her in her weaknesses.

We commonly call these times of inactivity "deserts." They occur when God draws us apart for a season, as he did with Moses (Exodus 2) and Beryl, and strips us of our busyness and our ability to operate in our strengths. He has not abandoned us, and he is not judging us. These can be precious times when we listen to God with new intensity. In these times we recognize anew our dependency on him, and our intimacy with him is deepened. This deep relationship must be our foundation if we are to fully embrace our destiny in Jesus Christ.

Are you in a desert experience? What can you do to deepen your intimacy with God in this situation?

5. Jesus repeats a certain instruction several times in verses 4–10. What does this instruction mean practically in your life?

6. Given what Jesus says in verse 5, why is it necessary to "remain" in him?

In what ways might your life be different if this truth were continually being worked out in you?

7. In verses 9–15, identify the parallels between our relationship with Jesus and his relationship with the Father.

Why do you think Jesus highlights these parallels?

A Vessel of Pure Gold

In the process of obtaining pure gold, a refiner's fire will expose the dross. In a similar way difficulties may lay bare our character weaknesses, which up to that point could well have remained hidden. Don't ignore what the fires of life expose, for even though they reveal truths about yourself that may be hard for you to receive, it is vital information. God's intention is to remove obstacles that keep you from experiencing abundant life.

So instead of trying to avoid the heat, let God use it in your life. Embrace the opportunity. Humility and teachableness in this situation will increase your spiritual growth. As we join in partnership with God, these character weaknesses will be transformed from crude ore into a vessel of pure gold that reflects his lovely image.

How have you responded to trials in the past? What character issues did they bring to the surface? How did you change?

8. Given how Jesus showed his love for you, how can you grow in loving others, both those who are easy to love and those who are not?

9. What does Jesus say are the things that distinguish friends from servants?

Do you feel more a servant of God or a friend of God? Why?

Think of an area in which you would like to grow more so that you can bear more fruit. Ask God to do what needs to be done, including pruning, to make that growth possible. Remember that God is with you in the whole process of pruning and bearing fruit.

god prunes those he loves so that they will grow and bear more fruit.

taking it further

Suggestions for application

DIGGING DEEPER

The Bible has much to say about our lives bearing fruit. See:

Psalm 1:3; Isaiah 32:17;
Romans 7:4;
Galatians 5:22–23.

Personal Expression

Draw up a timeline of your life, identifying in different colors times of pruning and the results of those times.

Meditation

Do you feel that you are in a time of pruning? Read Hebrews 12:5–11. In what way is God "disciplining" (pruning) you? Can you see why? Are you responding positively or negatively? Do you need to change your response? Talk to God about this. Take time to think about how this disciplining will produce righteousness and peace in your life.

Connecting to Life

Showing love to others is one of the fruits our lives can bear. Think of some people you desire to show love to in a practical way. Then consider how you might do that. Be creative. You could buy flowers for them, make a dinner, pray daily for them.

PEOPLE OF IMPACT

festo kivengere (1920—1988)

Death and disappearances were daily occurrences, but no one asked questions. Every word had to be carefully weighed and considered; rash words cost lives—which was why jaws dropped in shock as his words pierced the air in disregard of the officials present in the cathedral.

Whether they labeled him daring or foolhardy, none forgot the name of Festo Kivengere. In the midst of the dark years of torture and oppression under Idi Amin, Ugandan Christians found themselves with a bishop who would not be cowed into silence. His words were whispered on the streets: "Jesus Christ used his authority to save men and women. How are you using your authority? If you misuse the authority God gave you, God is going to judge you."

For all his courage in speaking out against the tyranny of his country's ruler, he became even better known for his proclamation, "I love Idi Amin." Only the life of Jesus could produce such an expression of compassion toward one causing so much suffering.

But Festo hadn't always shown the fruit of Christ's presence in his life; he had been raised to offer sacrifices to tribal gods. Encountering Jesus during the East African revival, he forsook the old gods forever. Festo was drawn to missions, serving as an evangelist in Tanzania and in his own country of Uganda and as an international speaker to crowds of thousands. Ordained by the Anglican church, Festo served Billy Graham as an interpreter in the 1950s and ministered with African Enterprise, an evangelistic outreach, as a team leader in the 1970s and 1980s.

Festo became a bishop in the church of Uganda during a time of intense turmoil in the country. Festo himself came under constant surveillance and was eventually forced to flee across the border into Rwanda—an exile lasting two years, primarily in the U.S. Upon Idi Amin's fall from power, the massive task of rebuilding his devastated country absorbed his energies but never overshadowed his vision for building a solid spiritual foundation in the lives of his people.

GUIDANCE — BEING LED BY GOD'S SPIRIT
Acts 16

"How can I know what God's will is?" The young man was curious, puzzled, and hungry for an answer, and he wasn't the only one. The group of young people at a Bible conference were gathered around the speaker for the weekend, and the question echoed what was in many of their hearts. The seasoned Bible professor smiled. "He'll let you know" was the confident reply. "He *wants* you to know — he's not trying to keep it from you."

The speaker's answer reveals what many of us fear: that for some reason God is hiding his will from us, and we have to convince him somehow to let us know what it is. But this Bible teacher knew God. He knew that God longs for us to know his will so that we can obey it.

"He goes on ahead of them, and his sheep follow him."

—JOHN 10:4

There are different ways in which God speaks to us and guides us, and we need to discern which way he is using at any given time. Sometimes we see people in the Bible struggling to find out exactly what it is God is saying. But as they seek him, learning to recognize his voice in the various ways in which he speaks, they discover God's will for them.

As you begin this study, ask that the Spirit of God will teach you more of what it means to be led by him.

- How do you know what God's will is?

- Describe some of the ways God has led you in the past.

engaging the text

setting the stage

- Paul is on his second missionary trip, accompanied by Silas who has replaced Barnabas.

- They plan to visit the churches planted on his first trip and are delivering a letter compiled by the first Jerusalem council for the churches.

- The Jerusalem council has made the definitive decision that Gentiles can become Christians without becoming Jews first.

- Paul normally visits the local synagogue of a new city to present the gospel there first.

- If the Jewish population of a city is too small to have a synagogue, the Jews normally meet outside the city walls.

- It is common practice among Gentiles to consult mediums and people possessed by a spirit for supposed guidance.

Read Acts 16

1. What are the different ways that God leads Paul in this chapter?

2. Why do you think Paul wants Timothy on his team (vv. 1–3)?

3. Can you think of an occasion when the recommendation of others or your own background were important factors in a decision you made? Describe that occasion.

4. Why does Paul not go to the provinces of Asia or Bithynia?

Learning to Listen

"Then the word of the LORD came to Samuel" (1 Samuel 15:10).

Learning to hear God's voice seems to come so easily for some people, while others struggle to hear a single word. There was a time when Samuel struggled to recognize the Lord's voice too. The first times God spoke to him Samuel thought it was Eli calling him (1 Samuel 3:4–8). Many of us hear the voice of the Lord but don't recognize it as his.

Learning to recognize the Lord's voice comes with practice. If we slow down and take time to listen, while also listening as others share godly wisdom with us (as Samuel heeded Eli's advice), we will grow in our ability to hear and to recognize God's voice. The important thing to remember is that God wants to communicate with us. From Genesis to Revelation we see him talking with his people. He wants us all to tune in. It's a vital part of the way we grow in our relationship with him and move into our destiny. Because he listened and responded obediently to both the encouraging and the hard words of God, Samuel was used to shape the destiny of Israel through what he heard and passed on to others.

Have you ever heard God speak to you? Spend time reading his Word and ask him to speak to you through it.

5. In verses 6–8, what are some of the ways you think the Spirit might have prevented Paul and his companions from going where they intended to?

6. Identify a time in your life when God stopped you from doing something in one way or another. How did you feel at the time?

7. What makes Paul decide to go to Philippi?

8. "God still speaks through visions and other supernatural means." Do you agree or disagree with this statement? Explain why.

Many people today seek supernatural guidance from horoscopes, mediums, channelers, and other occult sources. The Bible forbids any attempt to discover the future except through God himself. Why?

9. While Paul and his team are in Philippi, why do they go outside the gate and down to the river? (See also Setting the Stage.)

10. What do you think is the role of common sense and cultural customs in finding guidance from God?

11. Consider the events described in verses 19–34. Have you ever experienced hardship because you did the right thing or obeyed God's leading? What was your response to that hardship?

God has a plan for your life right now. Take time to ask him what it is. Come to him with the expectation that he desires for you to know his will and that he'll reveal it to you as you seek him.

those who are led by the spirit of god are sons of god.

Romans 8:14

taking it further
Suggestions for application

DIGGING DEEPER

To get a broader picture of what the Bible says about guidance, see:

2 Samuel 5:17–25; Psalm 119:105; Isaiah 48:17; John 10:1–6.

Connecting to Life

Begin a diary in which you record the times that you hear God, or draw up a timeline of your life and note the times when you heard God. Your faith will increase when you look back over everything God has said and done. For further insight into how God leads his people, read "Hearing the Voice of God" on page 93.

WORLD FOCUS

Many peoples of the world still seek help from spirits. Read about the Hausa people (on page 51) and pray that they would come to know the true God who can answer their prayers. It may be helpful to refer to the "Principles for Effective Intercession" on page 96.

PEOPLE PROFILE

the hausa — dark hopes for a hurting people

Location: West Africa. Population: 27 million. Religion: 99% Muslim.

Sokna hurried along wishing that her cousin, Bilkisu, would walk faster. They avoided using the dusty street where the men sat talking after the evening prayers at the mosque. Tonight Sokna was sure her dreams would be fulfilled. Having given birth to four daughters, Sokna was desperate for a son. But she believed she needed supernatural help if she was to give her husband a male child.

Both women stooped as they entered Tabara's doorway. Many women had already congregated and were busy discussing family concerns: a sickly child, an impending marriage, fear of divorce, a son approaching manhood. Tabara waved her hand and quieted the women. A hush fell over the group.

Excluded from the mosque, the women were about to turn to Bori spirits to help them solve their daily problems. Bori was the religion the Hausa practiced before the coming of Islam. Tabara signaled for the drums to begin their incessant beat. Sokna cried out to the Bori spirits to come and fill her so she could conceive a son.

Neither Sokna nor the other Hausa women have ever heard of the living God — the God who gives life to the dead, opens barren wombs, gives sons to desperate mothers, and heals sickly children. In their hopelessness, Hausa women turn to spirits of darkness for help. If only they could know the God who longs to intervene in their lives.

Pray that:

- God, the true Spirit of life, would reveal himself to the Hausa people.
- Christians would use biblical stories in their witness to Hausa women: stories about God meeting the family concerns of Sarah, Rebekah, Hannah, and Elizabeth.
- The women who oversee the Bori ceremonies would be converted.

Gifted to Give
Romans 12

John had come out of a rough background. Even after he became a Christian, his self-image remained very low. After all, what had he to offer anyone when his own life was such a mess? But there was someone who saw him differently. Tom, one of the church elders, had been observing John, noticing his questions in Sunday school class and his developing study habits. "John," he said after church one day, "I think you have a teaching gift."

John was amazed. To think that someone like Tom, a respected leader, would take notice of him and encourage him that he had something to offer! A short time after this he was asked to help teach a Sunday school class. Nervous but excited, he took up the challenge and was surprised to find people in the class responding well to his lessons. As he matured in his faith, he was asked more and more to teach in the church. John had discovered that he was gifted.

We have different gifts.

——ROMANS 12:6

Every one of us in the church has been equipped by God with spiritual gifts. They are not possessions for our own private use but are given to us so that we can give to others. As members of a body of believers, we are called to use these gifts, in partnership with the Holy Spirit, to bless one another. And in doing so, we will find that we are richly blessed ourselves.

As you work through this study, ask the Holy Spirit to show you more of how he has gifted you to minister to others.

PREPARING HEART AND MIND

- When you think of "gifted" people, what usually comes to your mind?

- How do you believe that God has gifted you to minister to others?

- What gifts do you think you might have that are lying dormant?

Read Romans 12

- Rome is the capital city of the Roman Empire and maintains its rule by ruthless use of power.

- Sexual immorality is the norm, modeled by the emperors themselves.

- Nero is emperor at this time; he later instigates the first Roman persecution of Christians.

- Paul is writing to the church in Rome, which is composed mostly of Gentile believers.

- Paul has never been to Rome, but is personally acquainted with many of the members of the church (see the long list of people in Romans 16).

- Paul appears to be seeking their support for further missions work (Romans 15:24).

1. What do you think Paul means by his instruction to the Roman believers in verse 1?

2. In verse 2, how does Paul suggest that there is a radical difference between the values of this world and God's values?

3. In what ways does your life reflect this radical difference?

4. Paul emphasizes a particular character quality in verses 3, 10, and 16. How do you think this contrasts with the way the world views "gifted" people? (Consider your responses to the questions in Preparing Heart and Mind.)

5. What do you think Paul's purpose is for the particular illustration he uses in verses 4–5?

Gifts of the Holy Spirit

God loves diversity, and that love is reflected in the gifts he's given to his people. He has imparted a variety of ministry gifts to serve the church's various needs. The beauty of this diversity is the wonderful unity within it. God intends that all the gifts of the Holy Spirit work in harmony. When the church is experiencing them all, its members also get a bigger picture of Jesus. Each gift reveals a different dimension of God's divine character. Through them we can see God's wisdom, his knowledge, his power, his healing, and many other aspects.

Though these are gifts, they are not ours to keep. They are to give away as the Holy Spirit leads, for the good of all. With this motivation of service in mind, Paul encourages us to "eagerly desire spiritual gifts" (1 Corinthians 14:1).

What spiritual gifts do you see at work in your church or in your friends? Which would you like to see at work in your life?

6. For each of the gifts listed (vv. 6–8) imagine what part of the body it could correspond to—for instance, the gift of prophecy could correspond to the tongue. Consider what it would be like to lose each of those parts of your physical body.

7. What do you think might be missing from Christ's body if you weren't a part of it?

8. Consider how we came to have our particular gifts. (Did we work for them; pay for them; receive them as a reward?) What does this tell us about how we are to use them?

9. What does Paul repeatedly instruct the believers in Rome to do with the gifts he mentions?

10. What might be holding you back from exercising the gifts God has given you?

Does Character Count?

We are understandably shocked to learn of the hidden sin of a church leader or evangelist. But Samson, the leader of his nation, visited a prostitute and a few hours later, God gave him supernatural strength to escape a trap. Why does the Holy Spirit continue to use such people?

We have to admit that God uses imperfect people. Otherwise none of us would qualify. The truth of the matter is this: When God uses someone, it's not a sign of his approval of their lifestyle but of his mercy on the people being served.

God's desire is to restore the Samsons, but in the absence of repentance he will allow them to experience the painful consequences of their sin. God did restore Samson's strength, but at the cost of his own life.

Ask God to reveal character weaknesses in your own life. Then invite the Holy Spirit to show you how to make changes in these areas.

11. Identify a time when you were blessed by someone using one of these gifts, and when you blessed someone else by using a gift.

Can you identify a time when someone used a gift and it wasn't a blessing? What made the difference?

12. Why do you think Paul gives instructions about character qualities (vv. 9–21) in this context of spiritual gifts?

13. What character qualities listed by Paul would you particularly like to grow in?

Ask the Lord to help you understand more of what your spiritual gift is and for the grace to use it. Also ask him to develop his character in you so that you will be able to use it wisely.

each one should use whatever gift he has received to serve others.

1 Peter 4:10

taking it further

Suggestions for application

DIGGING DEEPER

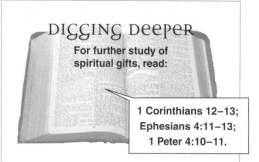

For further study of spiritual gifts, read:

1 Corinthians 12–13;
Ephesians 4:11–13;
1 Peter 4:10–11.

Connecting to Life

Choose one of the following projects that most appeals to you. As you find what you like to do best, you may discover your gift.

- Volunteer to fill an area of practical service in your church.
- Volunteer to teach a Sunday school class.
- Visit someone who is sick or in need.
- Give a word of encouragement to at least one person each day for a week.
- Give a financial gift above what you would normally give.
- Ask the Lord to give you an opportunity to serve in a leadership role.

Personal Expression

Cut out pictures and phrases from magazines and create a collage of how you could strengthen the body of Christ through your gifts. Take time to let God speak to you through what you have created.

People of Destiny—
Born for a Purpose
Genesis 12; 13; 15:1–6

Rejected! The word mocked her. Her missionary application had been barely looked at. It wasn't just being a single woman that worked against her but also racial prejudice and narrow assumptions on who constituted a missionary. Eliza became familiar with the bitter taste of disappointment, but she persisted in her dream to serve Jesus Christ in Africa.

Ten years passed before her hope was rewarded, and Eliza Davis-George departed for Liberia, a nation started by former slaves. During her fifty-five years in Africa, she saw thousands of Liberians come to faith in Jesus Christ, and she planted over a hundred churches. The years also held many struggles and disappointments: her battle for African souls; her husband, who broke under the emotional strain and died through alcohol abuse; the mission board, which often wavered in their support. But Eliza refused to give up, secure in the One who had called her for a purpose. She continued working in Liberia well into her nineties, the first black woman to pioneer missions in Africa.

> **"I will bless you . . . and you will be a blessing."**
>
> **—Genesis 12:2**

God has created each of us with a destiny, one that will both bless us and make us a blessing, whether in our own neighborhood or in the remote ends of the earth. However, entering into that destiny takes perseverance in the face of disappointments. God is bigger than the obstacles people may put in our path, as Eliza discovered. Our destiny may require our seeking forgiveness for our own failures and sins. God is able to forgive our failures, as Abraham discovered. If we are faithful, God will fulfill his destiny for us in the face of the most impossible circumstances.

- What do you think is the purpose of your life?

- In what ways are you achieving that?

- Does your destiny feel far away or just around the corner?

- What do you feel is preventing you from fulfilling your dreams?

engaging the text

setting the stage

- Abram is a pagan at the time God calls him (see Joshua 24:2–3).

- Ur is one of the major cities and cultural centers of the day. Ur's chief god is the moon god.

- Abram leaves Ur and its culture for a nomadic shepherd's life.

- Abram is the patriarch (absolute leader) of this nomadic community. As such, he has first choice of land and goods.

- It is shameful to be childless in the culture of the time.

- Abram's name, meaning "high father," is later changed to Abraham (Genesis 17:1–8), meaning "father of a multitude."

Read Genesis 12

1. If you were Abram, what would you find most difficult to leave behind?

2. God makes some amazing promises to Abram in verses 1–3. Try to put yourself in his place. How would the world around him change if he were to obey God?

How would his personal world change?

3. What difference would it make in your life if you knew God had a specific calling and destiny for you?

4. What do you think is wrong with what Abram does in verses 10–13?

5. Describe a time when you failed God in some way, but you saw that he continued to be faithful to you.

Read Genesis 13

6. What rights does Abram give up when his herdsmen argue with those of Lot? (See also Setting the Stage.)

Why do you think he dares to do this?

7. Why do you think God appears to him at this specific time with the particular promise in verses 14–17?

8. As with Abram, there are times that trusting God means we need to take a risk. This might mean giving up our rights in a particular situation, risking a friendship, hopes for the future, a job opportunity, or something else important to us. Can you think of such a time in your life? Describe it and what the result was.

Holding On to Our Dreams

God gives skills, abilities, and gifts to every person, and he wants us to develop them for his purposes. Unfortunately, life's obstacles cause many of us to give up on our own career and ministry dreams before they ever produce the fruit God intended.

Juan faced a major obstacle while in film school in his native Argentina. He felt God was calling him to make Christian videos, but the institute's third-year project required him to work on a film that promoted homosexuality. To continue in school meant compromising his beliefs; to drop out entailed possibly losing his vision. Though he had no other prospects, Juan left film school. For two years he kept pursuing his goal by reading all that he could. Then he heard about a new video production school offered in Hawaii by Youth With A Mission's University of the Nations. God opened the way for Juan to go, and now he's living out his vision.

God honors those who remain faithful in their calling. Once God gives us a vision, he may call us to lay it down for a season, but we must never give up on it.

What occupational direction has God given you? What tests of faith and integrity have you had to endure in pursuing it?

Read Genesis 15:1–6

9. In verse 1, God repeats some of his earlier promise, but omits what is probably the most important part to Abram. Why do you think he does this?

10. How does God's destiny for Abram also fulfill the desire of Abram's heart? (See also Setting the Stage.)

11. In what ways do *you* talk to God about the things which are most important to you?

12. You may be thinking that God has not fulfilled your heart's desire, and you are disappointed. What have you learned, or what are you learning, about God through this experience?

Embracing Disappointment

What does it mean to "rejoice in our sufferings" (Romans 5:3)? It's not trying to avoid them or pretending they don't exist. It's not even gritting our teeth in quiet submission to our circumstances. It means to embrace every situation, even the kind of unbearable turmoil and disappointment that Abraham felt in his childlessness. God calls his people to rejoice, not in spite of tribulation, but because of it. To the world this response would seem insane. But it is the most reasonable thing we can do when we understand what immeasurable benefits tribulation brings to us.

There is no greater witness in the world than that of Christians who endure, who truly embrace God's will for their lives and overcome everything the world and devil can throw at them. Making these things work for us and not against us is the key to real faith and real spiritual warfare.

Have there been difficult times in your life when you questioned God's love, wisdom, or power? How can you "consider it pure joy" (James 1:2) in the middle of difficult circumstances? How will this affect your behavior and thought life?

Responding to God

When God promises to give him a son and a multitude of descendants in Genesis 15:4–5, "Abram believed the Lord, and he credited it to him as righteousness" (v. 6). Abram responded in faith to the promise of God to fulfill his destiny. What dreams and hopes do you have for your future? Bring them to the Lord, asking him to reveal his purposes for you. Is there a response of faith that he is asking you to make now? Be prepared to take the risk and trust him.

NO eye Has seen,
NO ear Has HearD,
NO mind Has conceived
what god has
prepared
for those who love him.

1 Corinthians 2:9

taking it further
Suggestions for application

DIGGING DEEPER

For further encouragement and insight concerning your purpose, read:

> **Jeremiah 29:11;**
> **Ephesians 2:10;**
> **Philippians 2:5–11.**

Connecting to Life

Write your own obituary as if you had obeyed and fulfilled God's plan for your life. What would you like to be remembered for?

Personal Expression

Make a collage or drawing of where you have come from and where you think you are going in your life. Take time to pray, offering this creative expression to God as a way of telling him your heart's desires and committing them to him.

WORLD FOCUS

Read about the Bene-Israel people group on the next two pages, and pray for them that they would come to know the blessing of Abraham. Using the "Principles for Effective Intercession" (page 96) may be helpful for you as you pray.

PEOPLE PROFILE

bene-israel—an ancient people in need of the new covenant

Location: Bombay, India. Population: 12,000. Religion: 100% Jewish.

Abaji (Abraham) smiled as he carefully handed Bunnaji to the *Hazan*. The *Hazan* had officiated at this synagogue for many years, and Bunnaji was about to become one of countless boys he had circumcised. It was eight days since Bunnaji's (Benjamin's) birth—and the first day he had been permitted out of the home. Rikva, his mother, was prevented by custom from attending the circumcision.

Three chairs had been carefully arranged for the ceremony. The first had a copy of the Old Testament Scriptures on it and was reserved for the prophet Elijah—believed by the Bene-Israel to be the unseen guest present at every circumcision. The second was for the *Hazan,* and the third for the *sandek* (godfather), Abaji.

As he reached for the knife, the *Hazan* intoned prayers: "*B'shem Adoni*" (In the name of God). Bunnaji's wail pierced the hushed synagogue. With one sharp stroke of the knife Bunnaji had entered the Bene-Israel community.

This particular Jewish community traces its origin back hundreds of years to a time when their forefathers settled in Bombay. Some claimed they migrated from Babylon after the exile (2 Kings 25:11); others believed they were descendants of shipwrecked Yemeni Jews around the seventh century. Although their arrival in India has been lost in the mists of time, the age-old traditions of the Jews are as central in the community today as they have always been.

The Bene-Israel understand the old covenant and circumcision as a sign of covenantal relationship with God. But few have heard of the new covenant, which God established in Jesus Christ. They faithfully follow rituals that "are a shadow of the things that were to come; the reality, however, is found in Christ" (Colossians 2:17).

Pray that:

- The Bene-Israel would have the opportunity to hear of the new covenant from local Indian Christians.
- They would grasp what it means to be circumcised in heart and not just in the flesh (Jeremiah 4:4; Colossians 2:11).
- The Holy Spirit would reveal Christ through the traditions and the law of the Bene-Israel: "The law was put in charge to lead us to Christ that we might be justified by faith" (Galatians 3:24).

Leader's Notes

Leading a Bible study—especially for the first time—can make you feel both nervous and excited. If you are nervous, realize that you are in good company. Many biblical leaders, such as Moses, Joshua, and the apostle Paul, felt nervous and inadequate to lead others (see, for example, 1 Corinthians 2:3). Yet God's grace was sufficient for them, just as it will be for you.

Some excitement is also natural. Your leadership is a gift to the others in the group. Keep in mind, however, that other group members also share responsibility for the group. Your role is simply to stimulate discussion by asking questions and encouraging people to respond. The suggestions below can help you to be an effective leader.

The Role of the Holy Spirit

Always remember that the work of the Holy Spirit is necessary in order for each of us to understand and apply God's Word. Prayer, your prayer for one another, is critical for revelation to take place. You can be assured that God is working in every group member's life. Look for what is stirring in people's hearts. Listen to their statements and questions, and be aware of what they do not say as well as what they do say. Watch God do his work. He will help you lead others and feed you at the same time. May God's blessing be with you.

Preparing to Lead

1. Ask God to help you understand and apply the passage to your own life. Unless this happens, you will not be prepared to lead others.
2. Carefully work through each question in the study guide. Meditate and reflect on the passage as you formulate your answers.

3. Familiarize yourself with the leader's notes for the session. These will help you understand the purpose of the session and will provide valuable information about the questions.
4. Pray for the various members of the group. Ask God to use these studies to help you grow as disciples of Jesus Christ.
5. Before each meeting, make sure each person has a study guide. Encourage them to prepare beforehand for each study.

Leading the Study

Opening (approximately 5 minutes)

1. At the beginning of your first time together, take a little extra time to explain that the Living Encounters are designed for discussions, sharing, and prayer together, not as lectures. Encourage everyone to participate, but realize that some may be hesitant to speak during the first few sessions.
2. Begin on time. If people realize that the study begins on schedule, they will work harder to arrive on time. Open in prayer. You may then want to ask for feedback from one person who has followed through on the "Taking It Further" section from the previous week's study.
3. Read the introduction together. This will orient the group to the passage being studied.

Preparing Heart and Mind (approximately 15 minutes)

1. Although these questions may be considered by individuals beforehand, you are strongly encouraged to begin your group time with them. They are designed to provoke thinking about a topic that is directly related to the study. Anyone who wrestles with one or more of the questions will be better prepared to receive the truth found in the rest of the study.

2. If your time is very limited, encourage your group members to consider one or more of the questions before they arrive. It is not necessary to mention them in your meeting. However, you may want to ask for one person who has already considered the questions to share thoughts about one question with the group before moving on to "Engaging the Text."

Engaging the Text (approximately 50 minutes)

1. This section is a study of one or more passages of Scripture. Read the Scripture portion(s) aloud. You may choose to do this yourself, or you might ask for volunteers.
2. There are normally 10–12 questions, which will take the group through an inductive process of looking at the text. These questions are designed to be used just as they are written. If you wish, you may simply read each one aloud. Or you may prefer to express a question in your own words until it is clearly understood. Unnecessary rewording, however, is not recommended.
3. Don't be afraid of silence. People in the group may need time to think before responding.
4. Avoid answering your own questions. Even an eager group will quickly become passive and silent if they think the leader will do most of the talking.
5. Encourage more than one answer to each question. Ask, "What do the rest of you think?" or "Anyone else?" until several people have had a chance to respond.
6. Try to be affirming whenever possible. Let people know you appreciate their insights into the passage.
7. Never reject an answer. If it is clearly wrong, ask, "Which verse led you to that conclusion?" Or let the group handle the problem by asking them what they think about the question.

8. Avoid going off on tangents. If people wander off course, gently bring them back to the passage being considered.
9. End on time. This will be easier if you control the pace of the discussion by not spending too much time on some questions or too little on others.

Articles

There are several articles in each study that are set off by gray boxes. These offer additional information as well as help to liven up the group time. "Setting the Stage" relates directly to the study of the passage, and questions will refer you to this sidebar when needed. Other gray-boxed articles can further illustrate or apply a principle. Become acquainted with the articles beforehand so that you know what is available. Remember that reading one or more of these articles in the group will add to your meeting time.

Responding to God (approximately 10 minutes)

In every study guide a prayer response is built into the last few minutes of the group time. This is to allow for the Holy Spirit to bring further revelation as well as application of the truths studied into each person's life. Usually there is a suggested way to respond in prayer, but feel free to adjust that as you sense what God is doing.

Taking It Further

You may want to encourage people to do one or more of these suggestions during the week ahead. Perhaps ask one person to share about it at your next time together. Or, depending on your time constraints, you may choose to do some of these activities during your session together.

Many more suggestions and helps are found in the book *Leading Bible Discussions* (InterVarsity Press). Reading it would be well worth your time.

HOLINESS —— BEING LIKE HIM

Ephesians 4:17–5:20

Purpose: For participants to come to a deeper awareness that holiness does not mean keeping a set of rules. Rather, it means becoming more like God, reflecting his character in our lives, the character necessary for us to enter our true destiny. Through the study people will come to a better understanding of how to grow in holiness.

Engaging the Text

Question 1 People are enabled to connect the world of the Bible with their own world, to see that the issues Paul addresses "back then" are living issues today.

Question 2 Participants' understanding of holiness is moved away from the idea that it is something static. Paul's use of such language is an indication that we are to be *actively involved* in the process of change. There may be some in the group who will respond that they are "holy" because of Christ's righteousness. Don't cut off such comments, but be sure the group sees that, although it is true that we are "made holy" in Christ, there is also an active aspect to our growth in personal holiness. This is what Paul is emphasizing here.

Question 4 Some people may find it difficult to share their struggles. Don't force this in a group setting. However, there may be someone you know in the group who would be open to share, and this

could help others to be more open. Or you might do it yourself to set an example.

Question 5 People are helped to see that "holiness" is not an abstract thing
that affects only ourselves, but also has a very practical effect
on our relationships. Take time to let them examine the consequences of these changes.

Question 7 "In this matter of forgiving, the calling of Christians is to be followers of God. In fact, *mimetai* is more than followers. It is 'imitators' . . . a word used a number of times in the New Testament
for the following of a human example, but only here of imitating God Himself.

"Furthermore, the verb is more strictly 'become.' Those who by
grace are made children of God are by constant perseverance,
and by imitation of the divine copy (cf. 1 Peter 2:21) to become
more like the heavenly Father."[1]

Question 9 "Therefore, in the light of God's judgment and of the incom-
patibility of such sins with membership in the kingdom of God,
Paul calls on his readers not to be (literally 'become') partakers
with them. To join cause with such shameless sinners, with the
'sons of disobedience,' is an utter denial of their Christian pro-
fession, and the warning is implied that it involves the danger
of sharing the same consequences of sin in God's judgment."[2]

Question 12 This is a natural place to lead into a prayer time of response.

Responding to God

Use these suggestions as guidelines for prayer. One way to do this would be
to divide the group into twos or threes so they can share and pray for one
another. Alternatively, people could pray at home alone. Either way, encourage people to be specific about the areas in which they desire to grow.

Taking It Further

Refer to the explanation of this section in the introduction to the Leader's Notes. While not a requirement, the aim of these suggestions is to help the study have a continuing effect on lives through the following week. Encourage people to choose one or more of the activities which appeal to them. Make it clear that they are not expected to follow through on all the suggestions.

Contentment and Gratitude—
Keys to Peace of Mind

Philippians 3–4

Purpose: To encourage participants to make giving thanks and contentment a greater part of their lives, as well as to help them see God's care and involvement in their lives, whatever their circumstances are. They will also be challenged to examine their attitude toward finances and giving.

Engaging the Text

Question 2   William Hendriksen breaks into two categories those things in which Paul placed his confidence before coming to Christ. Such a breakdown, below, may be helpful for people to consider.

1. "What my parents gave me—circumcised on the eighth day; of the people of Israel; of the tribe of Benjamin; a Hebrew of Hebrews.

2. "What I, through my own efforts attained—as to the law a Pharisee; as to zeal persecuting the church; as to legal righteousness having become blameless."[3]

Question 3   Paul's language here is very strong. It is possible that some people will want to soften it. Try to keep the focus on the fact that Paul sees *no* value in putting confidence in the things in which he previously placed his trust.

Question 5 They are looking for their security and contentment in earthly things.

Question 7 "He says, Rejoice in the Lord always; again I will say, Rejoice. . . . Can one truly rejoice when the memory of past sins vexes the soul, when dear ones are suffering, when one is being persecuted, facing possible death? But there is Paul, who does, indeed, remember his past sins . . . whose friends are really suffering . . . who is even now a prisoner facing possible death; yet, who rejoices and tells others to do likewise."[4]

If it does not come up in the discussion, it may be appropriate to mention that part of Paul's encouragement is that "the Lord is near." When we go through difficult times it makes all the difference to be aware that God is with us.

Question 8 It may be that no one in the group can actually think of such a time in their lives, although normally in a group of Christians with a range of experiences and ages, there will be some. Examples could be when they have faced danger or the death of a loved one. An alternative possibility is to discuss situations where they would have *liked* to experience that peace. It is important that people's expectation is raised that they will meet God as they go through difficult times.

Question 9 What we focus on has a powerful effect on our ability to be content and to give thanks. People are helped to make the connection between the things Paul mentions and what happens in their own lives, and to consider what it is that they think about in difficult times. They are challenged to move from thinking, "What a nice bunch of things Paul writes," to asking themselves, "Am I doing what Paul says?"

Question 10 Finances can be a very sensitive issue for some people to discuss. Be aware of possible reactions. Some might feel defensive, while others might feel that many Christians don't give enough. Tithing may come up as a matter of controversy, but it is not the point here. The aim is to help people get a grasp on the issue of contentment with what we have. Look also for an opportunity to lead the discussion into encouraging generosity.

Question 12 Paul sends greetings from the saints of "Caesar's household." Although the Scriptures do not tell us for certain, it is generally accepted that members of Caesar's palace staff probably came to Christ through Paul's influence while he was imprisoned there. If this is so, we see that his life continued to have tremendous impact, even among those who were his jailers. One can almost imagine the jailer smiling and remembering when he hears the letter read!

THAT YOU MAY BE FRUITFUL

John 15:1–17

Purpose: That participants may become more aware of God's work in their lives, understand better the process of pruning, and become more fruitful for him.

Engaging the Text

Question 1 People are challenged to think about what Jesus is getting at in using these figures of speech, rather than simply accepting them without grasping their significance. It is important to realize that there is a dynamic relationship between Jesus, the Father, and each one of us, and that God is actively involved in the events of our lives.

Question 2 This is not a discussion about whether or not people can lose their salvation. People are helped to realize that bearing fruit is something that is required of them. Keep the discussion on a personal level: what does this mean for them specifically?

Leon Morris writes of this verse: "We should not regard this as a proof that true believers may fall away. It is part of the viticultural picture, and the point could not be made without it. The emphasis is on the bearing of fruit. Pruning is resorted to to ensure that this takes place."[5]

Question 4 Encourage people to actively reflect on what God is doing in their lives right at this moment and to describe it. One season is not better than another. Both are needed at different times in our lives.

Questions 5 to 7 "Remain in me" (often translated as "Abide in me"). People are helped to consider what they can do practically to remain in Jesus, to be more aware of his presence, so that what Jesus is describing here begins to become more than a nice religious phrase.

Question 7b See especially verse 11. Jesus' purpose is for us to know his joy.

Question 9 Encourage people to be honest with their feelings here. What is shared can become part of the prayer for one another (see below).

Responding to God

This is a suggested subject for prayer to close off the session. However, for some it might be more appropriate to deal with what has come out of question 9: that they would experience more of what it means to be a friend of Jesus, responding to him and his commands (v. 14) and so eventually bearing fruit for him. The point is that people would pray for God to continue his process in them so that they can bear more fruit.

session four

Guidance——Being Led by God's Spirit
Acts 16

Purpose: For participants to increase in their understanding of the ways in which God leads, to learn to become more sensitive to his guidance in their lives, and to develop confidence in their ability to hear God's voice, however he speaks.

Engaging the Text

Question 1 People are helped to recognize that there is a wide variety of ways in which God leads. God does not have only one method of guidance but speaks in a variety of ways.

Question 2 and 3 Timothy's mixed background has obvious advantages in relating to and reaching out to others. He is also recommended to Paul by his church. Sometimes part of God's guidance includes natural circumstances or the input of other people. However, it is possible that this will bring back painful memories for some people, when they didn't get a recommendation they had hoped for, or someone gave a bad report about them. Don't discourage this side of the picture. If it should come up, it may be helpful to have them consider it in the light of question 6.

Question 4 Bythinia is to the north of their route, and the Spirit of God would not allow them to go there. This answer could also be expanded on with the consideration that the Spirit was in the process of directing them toward Macedonia and Europe. One thing that can be pointed out from this section is that discovering God's will is sometimes a process rather than one event.

Question 5 "The missionary journeys of Paul exhibit an extraordinary combination of strategic planning and keen sensitiveness to the guidance of the Spirit of God, whether that guidance took the form of inward prompting or the overruling of external circumstances. This combination is specially noteworthy in the present passage. . . . Before crossing the regional frontier the party had been forbidden by the Holy Spirit (speaking perhaps through a prophet in the church at Lystra) to preach the gospel in the province of Asia—from which we may infer that their original plan had been to do this very thing, making for Ephesus by the Maeander valley. The Spirit, we may observe, gave them ample warning to change their plans. If the province of Asia was not to be the field of their evangelistic activity for the present, then it was natural for them to cast their eyes farther north, and think of the highly civilized province of Bythynia in North-West Asia Minor, with its Greek cities (of which Nicomedia and Nicaea were the most important) and Jewish colonies. . . .

"In saying that this second prohibition was imposed by "the Spirit of Jesus" (v. 7), whereas the former one is ascribed to "the Holy Spirit"(v. 6), Luke poses an interesting theological question. One and the same Spirit is intended, of course, but is there any significance in the change of phraseology? Possibly the methods used to communicate the Spirit's will on the two occasions were different: it may be that on the second occasion the communication took a form closely associated with the exalted Christ."[6]

Question 6 People are given the opportunity to express disappointment over times when God prevented them from doing something. As they consider what happened to them in the light of what happened to Paul, they may begin to see what they may not have realized before: that God had a better purpose for them than what they had considered at the time. When Paul was prevented from going to one place, it actually meant that God was directing him elsewhere.

Question 8   There may be different views about this question in your group. Some people may have experienced these forms of guidance. Give the freedom for all to share their views. You could also point out that, as seen in this passage, even though God still speaks by supernatural means, he also uses a lot of other methods to communicate to us.

Question 11   This could generate a wide variety of answers, for example: a teenager who was rejected because she wouldn't get drunk with her friends; the businessman who got in trouble with his boss because he wouldn't be dishonest in some business deal. Encourage people to see that obedience doesn't always mean lack of difficulties, but it does mean peace with God.

Hot Topic: To give some biblical reasoning as to why such occult practices are forbidden, see Deuteronomy 18:9–13. Also in Deuteronomy 13:4, in discussing the subject, Moses says, "It is the Lord your God you must follow, and him you must revere." His concern is that such practices lead us away from the Lord. Occult practices can put us in contact with demonic spirits, which lead us into bondage.

Responding to God

This is an opportunity for people in the group to pray for one another, for the Lord to show them his will. Let them pray in small groups of two or three. Encourage them to spend some time in silence as well, asking the Lord to speak. You may want to point out that the article on "Hearing the Voice of God" (page 93) can be very helpful in learning to listen for his guidance.

session five

Gifted to Give
Romans 12

Purpose: To help people to discover more of their place in the body of Christ as well as the gifts the Holy Spirit has given them. They are also encouraged to step out in using these gifts.

Engaging the Text

Question 1 Paul urges them to offer their bodies as "living sacrifices." People are encouraged to consider what it really means to offer themselves as living sacrifices to God. It is easy to read these words and not stop to consider what they mean practically. God wants to use us, and we need to actively present ourselves to him so that he can do so.

Question 2 F. F. Bruce writes concerning this verse: "In view of all that God has accomplished for his people in Christ, how should his people live? They should present themselves to God as a 'living sacrifice,' consecrated to him. The animal sacrifices of an earlier day have been rendered forever obsolete by Christ's self-offering, but there is always room for the worship rendered by obedient hearts. Instead of living by the standards of a world at discord with God, believers are exhorted to let the renewing of their minds by the power of the Spirit transform their lives into conformity with God's will.

"Doctrine is never taught in the Bible simply that it may be known; it is taught in order that it may be translated into practice: 'if you know these things, blessed are you if you do them' (John 13:17). Hence Paul repeatedly follows up an exposition of doctrine with an ethical exhortation, the latter being linked to the former, as here, with the participle 'therefore'."[7]

Question 4   While Paul describes it differently in each verse, it is clear that the character quality is humility. This contrasts with the egotism and pride often displayed by "gifted" people in the world. The world, and too often even the church, also exalt obviously "gifted" people. But Paul says we are all gifted. In understanding this, we as Christians should have a different attitude.

Question 7   This can be a good place for people to encourage each other. Some people may not be able to see what would be missing if they were not there, but even if they can, others can share what they would miss if that person wasn't part of the group.

Question 8   Since our gifts come from God, they are not something we have produced, so we can't be proud of them. Because God has given them, we should take them seriously. You might like people to look at the parable of the talents (Matthew 25:14–30). God is with us as we exercise the gifts. Different people may have other answers.

Question 9   John Murray writes in his commentary on Romans 12: "If we consider ourselves to possess gifts we do not have, then we have an inflated notion of our place and function; we sin by esteeming ourselves beyond what we are. But if we under-estimate, then we are refusing to acknowledge God's grace and we fail to exercise that which God has dispensed for our own sanctification and that of others. The positive injunction is the reproof of a false humility which equally with over self-esteem fails to assess the grace of God and the vocation which distin-guishing distribution of grace assigns to each."[8]

In other words, we are to recognize and use our gifts for the benefit and blessing of others.

Question 11 It can be very up-building for people to hear, or to speak out for themselves, how their gifts may have blessed others. Encourage this positive sharing. For the second part of the question, advise people not to mention names in their examples of negative uses of the gifts. It can break down trust and build walls, when we want them to see themselves more and more as part of the same body of Christ. Examples should be kept brief, but it is also important to recognize that gifts can be used unkindly, with judgment or pride, instead of humility and love.

Taking It Further

Connecting to Life: For those who choose this activity, encourage them to give a report in the group at a later date, as to how their discovery process is going. Are they discovering their gifts as they try these projects?

People of Destiny——Born for a Purpose

Genesis 12; 13; 15:1–6

Purpose: For people to understand that God has a purpose, a destiny for their lives, and that he is working in the events of their lives, including their failures, to prepare them for that destiny. They will grow in their assurance that God cares about the things that matter to them.

Engaging the Text

Questions 1 and 2 People are helped to put themselves in the shoes of Abram (Abraham). He leaves the security of an advanced urban center for the life of a wandering shepherd. Yet he goes because God has spoken to him, a pagan. God promises to bless him, and that through him all the nations of the world will be blessed. Have people imagine what Abram might think that blessing would be. You could encourage them to read chapter 18 on their own at home to see one example of Abram's response to God's promise.

Question 4 Some may question whether he does in fact do anything wrong. It makes sense to go where there is food during the famine. Abram is using common sense to protect his life. Let such questions come. However, if it doesn't arise in the discussion, raise the question as to how godly it is for Abram to risk Sarai to Pharaoh's harem in order to save his own life. Does he need to save his life in that way, or trust God in a deeper way?

Question 6 As the patriarch of the family, Abram would have first choice of the land. He gives up that right to Lot. It seems that he has made progress in learning to trust God in a deeper way. To human eyes it might look as if he is risking God's promise, but Abram has the faith to leave that issue to God.

Question 7 People are encouraged in their own expectation that God will meet them as they take steps of faith, as he meets Abram here.

Question 9 There might be a number of different answers to this. The aim is that people begin to see that it is important for Abram to talk to God about those things which are most important to him. God is waiting for him to ask. He mentions everything else here—protection, reward—but not a son.

Question 11 and 12 These questions might bring out areas of hurt and disappointment in people as they identify times when God didn't give the answer they wanted. It may be appropriate to remind them that Abram spent years waiting to see the fulfillment of God's promise. It may also be good to mention the story of Ishmael here (Genesis 16–17), even though it is not in the section of Scripture we are studying. His birth must have seemed, at first, to be the answer to the "heart's desire" of Abram—but it is not the answer God intends.

Responding to God

This can be done in twos and threes in the group. For some people the issue may be too sensitive to speak of in a group yet, although you can pray generally for God's purposes to be fulfilled. For others, speaking out what is in their hearts may be the step of faith they need to take.

If you know the Lord, you have already heard his voice—it is that inner leading that brought you to him in the first place. Jesus always checked with his Father (John 8:26–29), and so should we; hearing the voice of the heavenly Father is a basic right of every child of God. The following are a number of ways of fine-tuning this experience:

1 Hearing God's voice is possible for you!

Don't make guidance complicated. It's actually hard not to hear God if you really want to please and obey him! If you stay humble, he promises to guide you (Proverbs 16:9). Here are three simple steps to help in hearing his voice:

- *Submit* to his lordship. Ask him to help you silence your own thoughts and desires and the opinions of others that may be filling your mind (2 Corinthians 10:5). Even though you have been given a good mind to use, right now you want to hear the thoughts of the Lord, who has the *best* mind (Proverbs 3:5–6).
- *Resist* the enemy, in case he is trying to deceive you at this moment. Use the authority that Jesus Christ has given you to silence the voice of the enemy (Ephesians 6:10–20; James 4:7).
- *Expect* your loving heavenly Father to speak to you. After asking your question, wait for him to answer. He will (Exodus 33:11; Psalm 69:13; John 10:27).

2 God speaks in different ways

Allow God to speak to you in the way he chooses. Don't try to dictate to him concerning the guidance methods you prefer. He is Lord—you are his servant (1 Samuel 3:9). So listen with a yielded heart; there is a direct link between yieldedness and hearing. He may choose to speak to you through *his Word*. This could come in your daily reading of the Bible, or he could guide you to a particular verse (Psalm 119:105). He may speak to you through an *audible voice* (Exodus 3:4), through dreams (Matthew 2), or through *visions* (Isaiah 6:1; Revelation 1:12–17). But probably the most common way is through the quiet *inner voice* (Isaiah 30:21).

3	**Acknowledge your sin before God**	Confess any sin. A clean heart is necessary if you want to hear God (Psalm 66:18).
4	**Revisit the scene of God's guidance**	Use the Axhead Principle (see 2 Kings 6). If you seem to have lost your way, go back to the last time you knew the sharp, cutting edge of God's voice. Then obey. The key question is, "Have you obeyed the last thing God has told you to do?"
5	**God can and will speak to you!**	Get your own leading. God will use others to confirm your guidance, but you should also hear from him directly. It can be dangerous to rely on others to get the word of the Lord for you (1 Kings 13).
6	**God will make it clear in his time**	Don't talk about your guidance until God gives you permission to do so. Sometimes this happens immediately; at other times there is a delay. The main purpose of waiting is to avoid four pitfalls: *pride*—because God has spoken to you; *presumption*—by speaking before you have full understanding; *missing God's timing and method*; and *bringing confusion to others*, who also need prepared hearts (Ecclesiastes 3:7; Mark 5:19; Luke 9:36).
7	**Be alert to the signs God provides**	Use the Wise-Men Principle (see Matthew 2). Just as the wise men individually followed the star and were all led to the same Christ, so God will often use two or more spiritually sensitive people to *confirm* what he is telling you (2 Corinthians 13:1).
8	**Discern true guidance from false guidance**	Beware of counterfeits. Of course you have heard of a counterfeit dollar bill. But have you ever heard of a counterfeit paper bag? No. Why not? Because only things of value are worth counterfeiting. Satan has a counterfeit of everything of God that is possible for him to copy (Exodus 7:22; Acts 8:9–11). Counterfeit guidance comes, for example, through Ouija boards, seances, fortune-telling, and astrology (Leviticus 19:26; 20:6; 2 Kings 21:6). The guidance of the Holy Spirit leads you closer to Jesus and into true freedom. Satan's guidance leads you away from God into bondage. One key test for true guidance: Does your leading follow biblical principles? The Holy Spirit never contradicts the Word of God. Confess any sin. A clean heart is necessary if you want to hear God (Psalm 66:18).

9 **Yield your heart completely to the Lord**

Opposition from humans is sometimes guidance from God (Acts 21:10–14). The important thing again is yieldedness to the Lord (Daniel 6:6–23; Acts 4:18–21). Rebellion is never of God, but sometimes he asks us to step away from our elders in a way that is not rebellion but part of his plan. Trust that he will show your heart the difference.

10 **God will reveal your calling**

Every follower of Jesus has a unique ministry (Romans 12; 1 Corinthians 12; Ephesians 4:11–13; 1 Peter 4:10–11). The more you seek to hear God's voice in detail, the more effective you will be in your own calling. Guidance is not a game—it is serious business where we learn *what* God wants us to do and *how* he wants us to do it. The will of God is doing and saying the right thing in the right place, with the right people at the right time and in the right sequence, under the right leadership, using the right method with the right attitude of heart.

11 **Stay in constant communication with God**

Practice hearing God's voice and it becomes easier. It's like picking up the phone and recognizing the voice of your best friend . . . you know that voice because you have heard it so many times before. Compare the young Samuel with the older man Samuel (1 Samuel 3:4–7; 8:7–10; 12:11–18).

12 **God wants a relationship with you!**

Relationship is the most important reason for hearing the voice of the Lord. God is not only infinite, but personal. If you don't have communication, you don't have a personal relationship with him. True guidance is getting closer to the Guide. We grow to know the Lord better as he speaks to us; as we listen to him and obey him, we make his heart glad (Exodus 33:11; Matthew 7:24–27).

Loren Cunningham © 1984

1 Praise God for who he is, and for the privilege of engaging in the same wonderful ministry as the Lord Jesus (Hebrews 7:25). Praise God for the privilege of cooperating with him in the affairs of humankind through prayer.

2 Make sure your heart is clean before God by having given the Holy Spirit time to convict, should there be any unconfessed sin (Psalm 66:18; 139:23–24).

3 Acknowledge that you can't really pray without the direction and energy of the Holy Spirit (Romans 8:26). Ask God to utterly control you by his Spirit, receive by faith the reality that he does, and thank him (Ephesians 5:18).

4 Deal aggressively with the enemy. Come against him in the all-powerful name of the Lord Jesus Christ and with the "sword of the Spirit"—the Word of God (Ephesians 6:17; James 4:7).

5 Die to your own imaginations, desires, and burdens for what you feel you should pray about (Proverbs 3:5–6; 28:26; Isaiah 55:8).

6 Praise God now in faith for the remarkable prayer meeting you're going to have. He's a remarkable God, and he will do something consistent with his character.

7 Wait before God in silent expectancy, listening for his direction (Psalm 62:5; 81:11–13; Micah 7:7).

8 In obedience and faith, utter what God brings to your mind, believing (John 10:27). Keep asking God for direction, expecting him to give it to you. He will (Psalm 32:8). Make sure you don't move to the next subject until you've given God time to discharge all he wants to say regarding this burden—especially when praying in a group. Be encouraged by the lives of Moses, Daniel, Paul, and Anna, knowing that God gives revelation to those who make intercession a way of life.

9	If possible, have your Bible with you should God want to give you direction or confirmation from it (Psalm 119:105).
10	When God ceases to bring things to your mind for which to pray, finish by praising and thanking him for what he has done, reminding yourself of Romans 11:36: "For from him and through him and to him are all things. To him be the glory forever! Amen."

A WARNING: God knows the weakness of the human heart toward pride. If we speak of what God has revealed and done in intercession, it may lead to committing this sin. God shares his secrets with those who are able to keep them. There may come a time when he definitely prompts us to share, but unless this happens, we should remain silent: "The disciples kept this to themselves, and told no one at that time what they had seen" (Luke 9:36). "Mary treasured up all these things and pondered them in her heart" (Luke 2:19).

Joy Dawson © 1985

We all have an opportunity to affect the course of history. If we pray with clean hearts, regularly and effectively, for the nations, we become history shapers. We are to pray for all nations and to focus primarily on the body of Christ, the church, as God intends her to shape the course of history. This ministry of intercession also prepares her for future authority in his eternal kingdom (2 Chronicles 7:14; Job 12:23; Psalm 2:8–9; Isaiah 56:7; Daniel 7:27; Revelation 2:26–29).

Here are twelve steps to help you pray more effectively.

1
Thank and praise God for who he is and for:
- The privilege of cooperating with him in prayer.
- His involvement already in the nation for which he is leading you to pray (Philemon 4–6).

2
Pray for an unprecedented outpouring of the Holy Spirit upon the church worldwide (Psalm 85:6; Isaiah 64:1–3):
- That God's people would see that there is no substitute for revival, pray persistently, and be prepared for it. Consider these biblical promises for revival: Psalm 102:15–16; Isaiah 41:17–20; 45:8; 52:10; 59:19; 61:11; Hosea 6:3b; Zechariah 10:1.
- That the church would receive revelation of God's awesome holiness and unfathomable love leading to deep repentance, especially of the sins of idolatry, apathy, and disobedience, resulting in a passionate love for the Lord.

3
Pray for unity in the Body of Christ:
- For revelation of the pride and prejudice that separates.
- That reconciliation would result; success depends on it (Matthew 12:25).
- That seeing their need for each other, they would honor and prefer one another.
- That their manifest unity would influence the lost to come to Jesus Christ (John 17:23).

4 Pray for leaders (Judges 5:2; Psalm 75:7; Proverbs 8:13–15; 29:18; Ephesians 4:11):
- For spiritual leaders to be raised up who understand the character and ways of God and fear him.
- To receive vision related to the extension of God's kingdom worldwide.
- For righteous leaders to be placed into all spheres of authority and influence (Proverbs 28:2).
- That God would convict unrighteous leaders, and if they persist in sin, overthrow them.

5 Pray that God's Word would have its rightful place:
- As the basis for laws, moral values, and behavior (Psalm 119:126).
- That preachers and teachers would get their messages from God's Word, and live them and teach them (Jeremiah 23:22; 1 Corinthians 4:16–17).

6 Pray that God's people would see that obedience is the key to the Christian life, that God's priorities would become theirs (Psalm 19:11–14; 34:1; Proverbs 8:13; Matthew 4:10, 19; 2 Corinthians 7:1):

- A life of worship, praise, and intercession.
- Time alone with God, getting to know him through his Word, and waiting on him for directions.
- Having a heart burdened for the lost and witnessing to them.
- A biblical understanding and practice of the fear of the Lord that would permeate every believer's life.
- Fulfilling the conditions to be empowered by the Holy Spirit (Ephesians 5:18).

7 Pray for children and youth:
- To have the chance to be born, hear the gospel, and know that God loves them—that deliverance and healing would come to the abused and neglected.
- That God would raise up anointed ministries to teach them the character and ways of God.
- For revival to come among them.

8 Pray for workers:
- To be sent to every nation and from every nation (Matthew 9:38; 28:19–20).
- That every believer would embrace the mandate, "Go to the nations," and seek the necessary grace to stay home if God so directs.

9 Pray for an increased effectiveness of the varied media ministries targeted to reach the lost.

10 Engage in spiritual warfare (Matthew 16:18):
- Against satanic attacks on both the church and the unsaved.
- Ask God to reveal principalities dominating nations and cities. Pray against them (Ephesians 6:12–13; James 4:7; Revelation 12:11).

11 Pray for spiritual awakening of the unconverted, motivating them to seek God:
- Salvation of unrighteous leaders.
- Radical conversions of most unlikely people, resulting in powerful ministries.
- Revelation to come to the ignorant and the deceived of Jesus' deity and claims, with resultant conversions.

12 Release faith:
- That your prayers are being answered (John 14:13; 16:24; 2 Peter 3:9)!
- That the nations will fear him. Praise God that he will rebuild his church and appear in his glory (Psalm 102:15–16).

Joy Dawson © 1990

WORLD Map

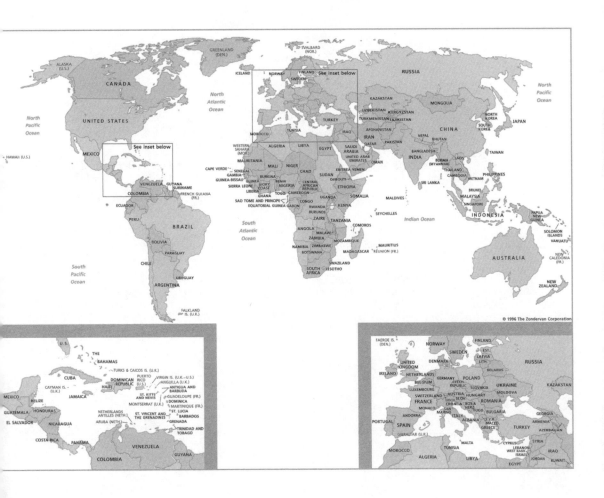

Notes

1. Francis Foulkes, *Tyndale New Testament Commentaries: The Epistle of Paul to the Ephesians* (Grand Rapids: Eerdmans, 1983), 138–39.

2. Ibid., 144.

3. William Hendriksen, *A Commentary on the Epistle to the Philippians* (Carlisle, Pa.: Banner of Truth Trust, 1962), 156–60.

4. Ibid., 192.

5. Leon Morris, *The Gospel According to John: The English Text with Introduction, Exposition and Notes* (Grand Rapids: Eerdmans, 1971), 669.

6. F. F. Bruce, *Commentary on the Book of the Acts: The English Text with Introduction, Exposition, and Notes* (Grand Rapids: Eerdmans, 1977), 325–27.

7. F. F. Bruce, *The Tyndale New Testament Commentaries: The Letter of Paul to the Romans: An Introduction and Commentary* (Grand Rapids: Eerdmans, 1985), 212.

8. John Murray, *The New International Commentary on the New Testament, The Epistle to the Romans: The English Text with Introduction, Exposition, and Notes* (Grand Rapids: Eerdmans, 1959), 117–18.

stay CONNECTED!

Living Encounters Series
Youth With A Mission

Styled after Youth With A Mission's (YWAM) successful Discipleship Training School (DTS), the Living Encounters series draws on YWAM's years of experience and expertise in training people of all ages for international ministry. Its unique, life-changing approach to Bible study will expand your small group's paradigm of Christianity . . . liberate its spiritual passion . . . and fill it with the joy and spiritual vigor that come from following an unpredictable, radical, and totally amazing risen Lord.

Experiencing the Spirit: *Living in the Active Presence of God*   0-310-22706-2
Seeing Jesus: *The Father Made Visible*   0-310-22707-0
Encountering God: *The God You've Always Wanted to Know*   0-310-22708-9
Building Relationships: *Connections for Life*   0-310-22709-7
Embracing God's Grace: *Strength to Face Life's Challenges*   0-310-22229-X
Expanding Your View: *Seeing the World God's Way*   0-310-22704-6
Making God Known: *Offering the Gift of Life*   0-310-22703-8
Finding Your Purpose: *Becoming All You Were Meant to Be*   0-310-22702-X

Look for Living Encounters at your local Christian bookstore.
ZondervanPublishingHouse

About Youth With a Mission

The Heart of Youth With A Mission

Youth With A Mission (YWAM) is an international movement of Christians from many denominations dedicated to presenting Jesus Christ personally to this generation, to mobilizing as many as possible to help in this task, and to training and equipping believers for their part in fulfilling the Great Commission. As Christians of God's Kingdom, we are called to love, worship, and obey our Lord, to love and serve his body, the Church, and to present the whole gospel for the whole man throughout the whole world.

We in Youth With A Mission believe that the Bible is God's inspired and authoritative Word, revealing that Jesus Christ is God's Son; that man is created in God's image; and that he created us to have eternal life through Jesus Christ; and that although all men have sinned and come short of God's glory, God has made salvation possible through the death on the cross and resurrection of Jesus Christ.

We believe that repentance, faith, love, and obedience are fitting responses to God's initiative of grace toward us; that God desires all men to be saved and to come to the knowledge of truth; and that the Holy Spirit's power is demonstrated in and through us for the accomplishing of Christ's last commandment: "Go into all the world and preach the good news to all creation" (Mark 16:15).

How Youth With A Mission Works

YWAM embraces three modes of action—ways which we believe God has given us to be a part of the goal of taking the gospel to all the world:

Evangelism — spreading God's message.
Training — preparing workers to reach others.
Mercy Ministries — showing God's love through practical assistance.

Youth With A Mission has a particular mandate for mobilizing and championing the ministry potential of young people. But our worldwide missions force also includes thousands of older people from all kinds of social, cultural, ethnic, and professional backgrounds. Our staff of 12,000 includes people from more than 135 nations and ranges from relatively new Christians to veteran pastors and missionaries.

We are committed to a lifestyle of dependence on God for guidance, financial provision, and holy living. We also affirm a lifestyle of worship, prayer, godly character, hospitality, generosity, servant leadership, team ministry, personal responsibility, and right relationships with one another and our families.

Because of its visionary calling, YWAM does new things in new ways where new initiatives are required. We seek to build bridges among Christian leaders, partnering with local churches and missions for completion of the Great Commission. Annually, over 35,000 people from various churches take part in YWAM's short-term outreach projects.

Teams from Youth With A Mission have now ministered in every country of the world and have ministry centers in 142 nations, but the work is far from complete. We welcome all who want to know God and make him known to join with us in finishing the task — to "make disciples of all nations" (Matthew 28:19).

for more information

For more information about YWAM, please contact YWAM Publishing to obtain YWAM's *Go Manual*, an annual directory of YWAM's addresses and training and service opportunities (send $5 to cover costs), or write one of our field offices for more information. Note: Please mention the Living Encounters Bible study series in your request for information.

YWAM Field Offices

Youth With A Mission
(The Americas Office)
P.O. Box 4600
Tyler, TX 75712 U.S.A.
1–903–882–5591

Youth With A Mission
(Europe, Middle East, & Africa Office)
Highfield Oval, Harpenden
Herts. AL5 4BX
England, U.K.
(44) 1582–463–300

Youth With A Mission
(Pacific & Asia Office)
P.O. Box 7
Mitchell, A.C.T. 2911
Australia
(61) 6–241–5500

YWAM International DTS
(Discipleship Training School) Centre
PF 608
Budapest 62
1399 Hungary
100726.1773@compuserve.com

YWAM Publishing

P.O. Box 55787
Seattle, WA 98155 U.S.A.
Phone: 1–800–922–2143 (U.S. only) or
1–425–771–1153
Fax: 1–425–775–2383
E-mail address:
75701.2772@compuserve.com
Web page:
www.ywampublishing.com

CHRISTIAN GROWTH STUDY BIBLE
New International Version

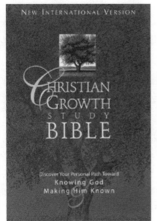

If you've enjoyed this YWAM study guide, you'll love this YWAM study Bible! The *Christian Growth Study Bible* is designed to help you cultivate heart-to-heart closeness with God. The kind you've longed for and God created you for. A dynamic, growing relationship so vital and life-changing that you can't keep it to yourself—you've got to tell the world about it and help others discover the greatness of your heavenly Father.

Knowing God and Making Him Known is the heartbeat of the *Christian Growth Study Bible*. It's also the heartbeat of Youth With A Mission (YWAM). Which is why this Bible's study program is modeled after YWAM's proven approach in their Discipleship Training Schools. At last, here's a study Bible with a 30-path program that will help you take the uncertainty out of your Christian growth. It helps you determine where you are on the path toward maturity—and helps remove the guesswork about where to go from there.

This *Christian Growth Study Bible* will be an invaluable tool for you to use with your Living Encounters Bible study series, giving you further help on the topics you will be exploring.

Hardcover	ISBN 0-310-91809X
	ISBN 0-310-918138 Indexed
Softcover	ISBN 0-310-918103
Black Bonded Leather	ISBN 0-310-91812X
	ISBN 0-310-918154 Indexed
Burgundy Bonded Leather	ISBN 0-310-918111
	ISBN 0-310-918146 Indexed

We want to hear from you. Please send your comments about this
book to us in care of the address below. Thank you.

ZondervanPublishingHouse
Grand Rapids, Michigan 49530
http://www.zondervan.com